★★★ THE ★★★ SCOUTER'S COMPANION

TIPS AND STORIES
CELEBRATING 100 YEARS

GIBBS SMITH
TO ENRICH AND INSPIRE HUMANKIND

First Edition
14 13 12 11 10   5 4 3 2 1

This is not an official publication
of the Boy Scouts of America.

Published by
Gibbs Smith
P.O. Box 667
Layton, Utah 84041

1.800.835.4993 orders
www.gibbs-smith.com

Designed by Kurt Wahlner
Printed and bound in the United States

Gibbs Smith books are printed on
either recycled, 100% post-consumer
waste, FSC-certified papers or on paper
produced from a 100% certified sustainable
forest/controlled wood source.

Library of Congress Cataloging-
in-Publication Data

The scouter's companion : tips and
stories celebrating 100 years. — 1st ed.
     p. cm.
  ISBN-13: 978-1-4236-0604-8
  ISBN-10: 1-4236-0604-3
  1. Boy Scouts of America 2. Boy Scouts—
United States. I. Gibbs Smith, Publisher.
  HS3313.S355 2010
  369.430973—dc22

                                    2009043150

Contents

Scouting, Exploring,
    and Camping 8
Service 40
God, Country, and Self 46
Trustworthiness 62
Loyalty 68
Helpfulness 72
Friendliness 80
Courteousness 90
Kindness 94
Obedience 100
Cheerfulness 106
Thriftiness 112
Bravery 118
Cleanliness 128
Reverence 134
Famous Scouts 141

Gen. Sir Robert Baden-Powell

Ernest Thompson Seton

Dan Beard

I had a vision for my people—a man of perfect manhood, a being physically robust, an athlete, an outdoorsman, accustomed to brunt of flood, wind and sun—rough road and open spaces—a man wise in the ways of the woods, sagacious in council, dignified, courteous, respectful to all, a good-natured giant; a man whose life was clean, picturesque, heroic and unsordid; a man of courage, equipped for emergencies, possessing his soul at all times, and filled with a religion that consists, not of mere occasional observances, not of vague merits hoarded in the skies, but of a strong kind spirit that makes him desired and helpful here today.

—ERNEST THOMPSON SETON
CO-FOUNDER OF
THE BOY SCOUTS OF AMERICA

Scouting, Exploring, and Camping

Young men, life is before you. Two voices are calling you—one coming out from the swamps of selfishness and force, where success means death; and the other from the hilltops of justice and progress, where even failure brings glory. Two lights are seen in your horizon—one the fast fading marsh light of power, and the other the slowly rising sun of human brotherhood. Two ways lie open for you—one leading to an even lower and lower plain, where are heard the cries of despair and the curses of the poor, where manhood shrivels and possession rots down the possessor; and the other leading to the highlands of the morning, where are heard the glad shouts of humanity and where honest effort is rewarded with immortality.

—John P. Altgeld
former United States governor

from *Camp Life*

Camp life means to live under canvas, away from the piles of brick and stone that we generally call our cities. It means to be in the open air, to breathe pure oxygen, to sleep upon "a bed of boughs beside the trail," to hear the whisper of the trees from amidst the fragrance of the "couch of boughs," to look at the camp fire and the stars when the sun has set, to

I go to nature
to be soothed
and healed,
and to have
my senses
put in order.

—JOHN BURROUGHS
ESSAYIST
AND ENVIRONMENTALIST

ply the oar or wield the paddle in the moonlight; to dive in the cool waters of the lake or river at dawn; to eat the plain substantial food of the forests and the wilds, with the delicacy of the fish and fruit which they afford; and to come heart to heart with nature in constant communion with the woods, the mountains, and streams—all of this is camping, and all of this is good.

A boy learns self-resourcefulness in this outdoor life faster than he would anywhere else; and somehow or other, every lake, and tree, and star, and pool of water come to be his personal friends, so that no matter where he is, he is never alone; and whether in solitude or with companions, he is cheerful and sunny and always ready to help others.

—John L. Alexander
writer and editor

Be prepared means you are always in a state of readiness in mind and body to do your duty:

Be prepared in mind by having disciplined yourself to be obedient to every order, and also by having thought out beforehand any accident or situation that might occur, so that you *know* the right thing to do at the right moment, and are willing to do it.

Be prepared in body by making yourself strong and active and *able* to do the right thing at the right moment, and to do it.

—Robert Baden-Powell
co-founder of the Boy Scouts of America

The Magic of the Campfire

What is a camp without a campfire?—no camp at all, but a chilly place in a landscape, where some people happen to have some things . . . When men sit together at the campfire they seem to shed all modern form and poise, and hark back to the primitive—to meet as man and man—to show the naked soul. Your campfire partner wins your love, or hate, mostly your love; and having camped in peace together, is a lasting bond of union—however wide your worlds may be apart. The campfire, then, is the focal centre of all primitive brotherhood. We shall not fail to use its magic powers.

—Ernest Thompson Seton
co-founder of the Boy Scouts of America

from *Man Packing*

Any uncomfortable pack is an abomination; too heavy a pack is an unhappy burden; no pack at all is fine—until you reach camp and hunt around for something to answer for a toothbrush, comb and brush, something on which to sit and sleep, something overhead to protect you from the rains and dews of heaven, something to eat and something to eat with besides your fingers, something from which to drink which holds water better than the hollow of your hand or the brim of your hat, and, in fact, all those necessary little comforts that a fellow wants on an overnight hike. Without these useful articles one will wish that he had subjected himself to the slight fatigue necessary to pack a small pack on his back.

—Daniel Carter Beard
co-founder of the Boy Scouts of America

from *Camping*

To many a city man there comes a time when the great town wearies him. He hates its sights and smells and clangor. Every duty is a task and every caller is a bore. There come visions of green fields and far-rolling hills, of tall forests and cool, swift-flowing streams. He yearns for the thrill of the chase, for the keen-eyed silent stalking; or, rod in hand, he would seek that mysterious pool where the father of all trout lurks for his lure.

—Horace Kephart
travel writer

In the woods, we return to reason and faith.

—Ralph Waldo Emerson
philosopher, poet, and essayist

This Land Is Your Land

CHORUS
This land is your land, this land is my land
From California, to the New York Island
From the redwood forest, to the Gulf Stream waters
This land was made for you and me.

As I was walking that ribbon of highway
I saw above me an endless skyway
I saw below me that golden valley
This land was made for you and me.

CHORUS

I've roamed and rambled and I followed my footsteps
To the sparkling sands of her diamond deserts
And all around me a voice was sounding
This land was made for you and me.

When the sun came shining, and I was strolling
And the wheat fields waving and the dust clouds rolling
As the fog was lifting a voice was chanting
This land was made for you and me.

As I went walking, I saw a sign there
And on the sign it said "No Trespassing"
But on the other side it didn't say nothing!
That side was made for you and me.

In the shadow of the steeple I saw my people
By the relief office, I seen my people
As they stood there hungry, I stood there asking
Is this land made for you and me?

Nobody living can ever stop me
As I go walking that freedom highway
Nobody living can make me turn back
This land was made for you and me.

**—Woody Guthrie
songwriter and musician**

There comes a time in every rightly constructed boy's life that he has a raging desire to go somewhere and dig for hidden treasure.

—MARK TWAIN
WRITER AND HUMORIST

from *My First Summer in the Sierra*

We are now in the mountains and they are in us, kindling enthusiasm, making every nerve quiver, filling every pore and cell of us. Our flesh-and-bone tabernacle seems transparent as glass to the beauty about us, as if truly an inseparable part of it, thrilling with the air and trees, streams and rocks, in the waves of the sun—a part of all nature, neither old nor young, sick nor well, but immortal. Just now I can hardly conceive of any bodily condition dependent on food or health any more than the ground or the sky. How glorious a conversion, so complete and wholesome it is, scarce memory enough of old bondage days left as a standpoint to view from! In this newness of life we seem to have been so always.

—John Muir
writer and environmentalist

The Boy Scouts of America stands for a set of principles. These principles have a lot of staying power. The values you learn as a Scout are like a compass. They can help you find your way through difficult and sometimes uncharted terrain. The principles of Scouting give you a sense of what's important.

—Bill Bradley
former United States senator

from *The art of Seeing Things*

The eye sees what it has the means of seeing, and its means of seeing are in proportion to the love and desire behind it. The eye is informed and sharpened by the thought. My boy sees ducks on the river where and when I cannot, because at certain seasons he thinks ducks and dreams ducks. One season my neighbor asked me if the bees had injured my grapes. I said, "No; the bees never injure my grapes."

"They do mine," he replied; "they puncture the skin for the juice, and at times the clusters are covered with them."

"No," I said, "it is not the bees that puncture the skin; it is birds."

"What birds?"

"The orioles."

"But I haven't seen any orioles," he rejoined.

"We have," I continued, "because at this season we think orioles; we have learned by experience how destructive the birds are in the vineyard, and we are on the lookout for them; our eyes and ears are ready for them."

If we think birds, we shall see birds wherever we go; if we think arrowheads, as Thoreau did, we shall pick up arrowheads in every field. Some people have an eye for four-leaved clovers; they see them as they walk hastily over the turf, for they already have them in their eyes. I once took a walk with the late Professor Eaton of Yale. He was just then specifically interested in the mosses, and he found them, all kinds, everywhere. I can see him yet, every few minutes upon his knees, adjusting his eye-glasses before some rare specimen. The beauty he found in them, and pointed out to me, kindled my enthusiasm also. I once spent a summer day at the mountain home of a well-known literary woman and editor. She lamented the absence of birds about her house. I named a half-dozen or more within an hour—the indigo-bird, the purple finch, the yellowbird, the veery thrush, the red-eyed vireo, the song sparrow.

17

Wilderness
is not a
luxury but
a necessity
of the
human spirit.

—Edward Abbey
WRITER AND ACTIVIST

"Do you mean to say you have seen or heard all these birds while sitting here on my porch?" she inquired.

"I really have," I said.

"I do not see them or hear them," she replied, "and yet I want to very much."

"No," said I; "you only *want to want* to see and hear them."

You must have the bird in your heart before you can find it in the bush.

I was sitting in front of a farmhouse one day in company with the local Nimrod. In a maple tree in front of us I saw the great crested flycatcher. I called the hunter's attention to it, and asked him if he had ever seen that bird before. No, he had not; it was a new bird to him. But he had probably seen it scores of times—seen it without regarding it. It was not the game he was in quest of, and his eye heeded it not.

Human and artificial sounds and objects thrust themselves upon us; they are within our sphere, so to speak; but the life of nature we must meet halfway; it is shy, withdrawn, and blends itself with a vast neutral background. We must be initiated; it is an order the secrets of which are well guarded.

—John Burroughs
essayist and environmentalist

To know what to do, and to "be prepared" to do it, is one of the privileges and duties and the glories of every Boy Scout.

—John L. Alexander
writer and editor

When I Heard the Learn'd Astronomer

When I heard the learn'd astronomer,
When the proofs, the figures, were ranged in columns
    before me,
When I was shown the charts and diagrams, to add, divide,
    and measure them,
When I sitting heard the astronomer where he lectured with
    much applause in the lecture-room
How soon unaccountable I became tired and sick,
Till rising and gliding out I wandered off by myself,
In the mystical moist night-air, and from time to time,
Look'd up in perfect silence at the stars.

**—Walt Whitman
poet**

Mountain Dew Song

My brother Bill runs a still on the hill
Where he turns out a gallon or two
And the buzzards in the sky get so drunk they cannot fly
Just from sniffing that good ol' mountain dew.

CHORUS
They call it that good ol' mountain dew,
And them that refuse it are few.
I'll hush up my mug if you fill up my jug
With that good ol' mountain dew.

My aunt Lucille had an automobile,
It ran on a gallon or two.
It didn't need no gas and it went awful fast
Running on that good ol' mountain dew.

My uncle Mort, he is sawed off and short,
He measures 'bout four foot two.
But he thinks he's a giant when you give him a pint
Of that good ol' mountain dew.

Chorus

My uncle Art, he ain't very smart,
His IQ is just twenty-two.
But he thinks he's a wizard
When he fills up his gizzard
With that good ol' mountain dew.

Chorus

There's an old hollow tree just a little way from me
Where you lay down a dollar or two.
If you hush up your mug, then they'll give you a jug
Of that good ol' mountain dew.

Chorus

—traditional

from *Walden*

I went to the woods because I wished to live deliberately, to front only the essential facts of life, and see if I could not learn what it had to teach, and not, when I came to die, discover that I had not lived. I did not wish to live what was not life, living is so dear; nor did I wish to practice resignation, unless it was quite necessary. I wanted to live deep and suck out all the marrow of life, to live so sturdily and Spartan-like as to put to rout all that was not life, to cut a broad swath and shave close, to drive life into a corner, and reduce it to its lowest terms, and, if it proved to be mean, why then to get the whole and genuine meanness of it, and publish its meanness to the world; or if it were sublime, to know it by experience, and be able to give a true account of it in my next excursion.

—Henry David Thoreau
writer and environmentalist

The Eagle

He clasps the crag with crooked hands;
Close to the sun in lonely lands,
Ring'd with the azure world, he stands.

The wrinkled sea beneath him crawls;
He watches from his mountain walls,
And like a thunderbolt he falls.

—Alfred Lord Tennyson
poet

We do not inherit the earth from our ancestors, we borrow it from our children.

—Navajo proverb

One touch
of nature
makes
the
whole
world
kin.

—WILLIAM SHAKESPEARE
POET AND PLAYWRIGHT

When Lost in the Woods

If you should miss your way, the first thing to remember is, like the Indian, "You are not lost; it is the teepee that is lost." It isn't serious. It cannot be so, unless you do something foolish.

The first and most natural thing to do is to get on a hill, up a tree, or other high lookout, and seek for some landmark near the camp. You may be so sure of these things:

You are not nearly as far from camp as you think you are.

Your friends will soon find you.

You can help them best by signaling.

The worst thing you can do is to get frightened. The truly dangerous enemy is not the cold or the hunger, so much as the fear. It is fear that robs the wanderer of his judgment and of his limb power; it is fear that turns the passing experience into a final tragedy . . .

In a word, keep cool, make yourself comfortable, leave a record of your travels, and help your friends to find you.

—Ernest Thompson Seton
co-founder of the Boy Scouts of America

I think the character that you learn in Scouting—working together, being honest with each other, being close knit . . . and depending on one another, on our camping trips and doing things—all these things build character in a young man that he takes with him into adulthood and makes him a much better citizen.

—James A. Lovell Jr.
former NASA astronaut

Home on the Range

Oh, give me a home where the buffalo roam,
Where the deer and the antelope play,
Where seldom is heard a discouraging word
And the skies are not cloudy all day.

CHORUS
Home, home on the range,
Where the deer and the antelope play,
Where seldom is heard a discouraging word
And the skies are not cloudy all day.

Where the air is so pure, the zephyrs so free,
The breezes so balmy and light,
That I would not exchange my home on the range
For all of the cities so bright.

CHORUS

How often at night when the heavens are bright,
With the light from the glittering stars,
Have I stood there amazed and asked as I gazed
If their glory exceeds that of ours.

CHORUS

Oh, give me a land where the bright diamond sand
Flows leisurely down the stream,
Where the graceful white swan goes gliding along
Like a maid in heavenly dream.

CHORUS

—Brewster M. Higley
medical doctor

Perhaps
the truth
depends
on a walk
around
the lake.

—WALLACE STEVENS
POET

Roadkill Stew

Sung to the tune of "Three Blind Mice"

Roadkill stew
Roadkill stew
Tastes so good
Just like it should

First you go down to the Interstate
You wait for the critter to meet its fate
You take it home and make it great
Roadkill stew
Roadkill stew

from *Pioneering*

Every Scout ought to be able to tie knots.

To tie a knot seems to be a simple thing, and yet there are right ways and wrong ways of doing it, and scouts ought to know the right way. Very often it may happen that lives depend on a knot being properly tied.

The right kind of knot is one which you can be certain will hold under any amount of strain, and which you can always undo easily if you wish to.

A bad knot, which is called a "granny," is one that slips away when a hard pull comes on it, or which gets jammed so tight that you cannot untie it.

—Robert Baden-Powell
co-founder of the Boy Scouts of America

from *Ulysses*

There lies the port; the vessel puffs her sail;
There gloom the dark, broad seas. My mariners,
Souls that have toiled, and wrought, and thought with me—
That ever with a frolic welcome took
The thunder and the sunshine, and opposed
Free hearts, free foreheads—you and I are old;
Old age hath yet his honor and his toil.
Death closes all; but something ere the end,
Some work of noble note, may yet be done,
Not unbecoming men that strove with gods.
The lights begin to twinkle from the rocks;
The long day wanes; the slow moon climbs; the deep
Moans round with many voices. Come, my friend.
'Tis not too late to seek a newer world.
Push off, and sitting well in order smite
The sounding furrows; for my purpose holds
To sail beyond the sunset, and the baths
Of all the western stars, until I die.
It may be that the gulfs will wash us down;
It may be that we will touch the Happy Isles,
And see the great Achilles, whom we knew.
Though much is taken, much abides; and though
We are not now that strength which in old days
Moved earth and heaven, that which we are, we are—
One equal temper of heroic hearts,
Made weak by time and fate, but strong in will
To strive, to seek, to find, and not to yield.

—Alfred Lord Tennyson
poet

Keep on the Sunny Side

There's a dark and troubled side of life
There's a bright and a sunny side too
Though we meet with the darkness and strife
The sunny side we also may view

CHORUS
Keep on the sunny side, always on the sunny side
Keep on the sunny side of life
It will help us every day, it will brighten all our way
If we keep on the sunny side of life

Oh, the storm and its fury broke today
Crushing hopes that we cherish so dear
Clouds and storms will in time pass away
The sun again will shine bright and clear

CHORUS

Let us greet with a song of hope each day
Though the moments be cloudy or fair
Let us trust in our Savior always
To keep us, every one, in His care

CHORUS

—Ada Blenkhorn

We must depend on the Boy Scout movement to produce the men of the future.

—Daniel Carter Beard
co-founder of the Boy Scouts of America

Thoughts come clearly while one walks.

—Thomas Mann
writer and Nobel Prize laureate

Climb the mountains and get their good tidings. Nature's peace will flow into you as sunshine flows into trees. The winds will blow their own freshness into you, and storms their energy, while cares will drop off like autumn leaves.

—John Muir
writer and environmentalist

How to Mount a Western Horse

Years ago when the rider was in Montana on Howard Eaton's Ranch, near the celebrated ranch of Theodore Roosevelt, he had his first experience with Western horses, and being sensitive and standing in great terror of being called a tenderfoot, he shyly watched the others mount before he attempted to do so himself. Each one of these plainsmen, he noticed, the reins in his left hand while standing on the left-hand side of the horse; then holding the reins over the shoulders of the horse he grasped the mane with the same hand, and put his left foot into the stirrup. But to put the left foot in the stirrup he turned the stirrup around so that he could mount while

Study nature,
love nature,
stay close
to nature.
It will
never
fail you.

—FRANK LLOYD WRIGHT
ARCHITECT AND WRITER

facing the horse's tail, then he grabbed hold of the pummel with his right hand and swung into the saddle as the horse started.

That looked easy; the writer also noticed that just before the others struck the saddle they gave a whoop, so without showing any hesitation the author walked up to his cayuse, took the reins confidently in his left hand, using care to stand on the left-hand side of the horse; then he placed the left hand with the reins between the shoulders of the horse and grabbed the mane, turned his back to the horse's head, put his left foot in the stirrup and gave a yell.

On sober afterthought he decided that he gave a yell too soon; the horse almost went out from under him, or at least so it seemed to him, or maybe the sensation would be better described to say that it appeared to him as if he went a mile over the prairie with his right leg waving in the air like a one-winged aeroplane, before he finally settled down into the saddle.

But this could not have been really true, because everybody applauded and the writer was at once accepted by the crowd without question as a thoroughbred Sourdough. Possibly they may have thought he was feeling good and just doing some stunts.

It may interest the reader to state that the author did his best to live up to the first impression he had made, but *he did not go riding the next day*, there were some books he thought necessary to read; he discovered, however, that he lounging was not without some discomfort; for instance, he could not cross his knees without helping one leg over with both his hands; in fact, he could find no muscle in his body that could be moved without considerable exertion and pain.

But this is the point of the story: Had the author tried to mount that cayuse in any other way he would have been left sprawling on the prairie. The truth is that if you mount properly when the horse starts, even if he begins to buck and pinch, the action will tend to throw you into the saddle, not out of it.

—Daniel Carter Beard
co-founder of the Boy Scouts of America

The best remedy for those who are afraid, lonely or unhappy is to go outside, somewhere where they can be quiet, alone with the heavens, nature and God.

—Anne Frank
author of *The Diary of a Young Girl*

Those who contemplate the beauty of the earth find reserves of strength that will endure as long as life lasts.

—Rachel Carson
writer and activist

I believe
a leaf
of grass
is no less
than the
journey-work
of the stars.

—WALT WHITMAN
POET

Red River Valley

Oh, they say that this valley you're leaving
We will miss your bright eyes and sweet smile
For you take with you all of the sunshine
That has brightened our lives for a while.

CHORUS
Then come sit by my side if you love me
Do not hasten to bid me adieu
But remember the Red River Valley
And the cowboy that loved you so true.

For a long time my darling I've waited
For those sweet words you never would say
Now, alas, all my fond hopes have vanished
And they say you are going away.

CHORUS

Will you think of this valley you're leaving
Oh, how lonely and dreary 'twill be
Will you think of the fond hearts you're grieving
And the pain you are causing to me?

CHORUS

I have promised you, darling, that never
Would a word from my lips cause you pain
And my life it will be yours forever
If you only will love me again.

CHORUS

Must the past with its sorrows be blighted
By the future of sorrow and pain;
Must the vows that were spoke be slighted;
Don't you think you could love me again?

CHORUS

There never could be such a longing
In the heart of a poor cowboy's breast
As dwells in the heart you are breaking
As I wait in my home in the west.

CHORUS

—traditional

Shenandoah
Oh, Shenandoah, I long to hear you,
Away, you rolling river
Oh, Shenandoah, I long to hear you
Away, I'm bound away, 'cross the wide Missouri.

Oh, Shenandoah, I love your daughter,
Away, you rolling river
Oh, Shenandoah, I love your daughter
Away, I'm bound away, 'cross the wide Missouri.

Oh, Shenandoah, I'm bound to leave you,
Away, you rolling river
Oh, Shenandoah, I'm bound to leave you
Away, I'm bound away, 'cross the wide Missouri.

Oh, Shenandoah, I long to see you,
Away, you rolling river
Oh, Shenandoah, I long to see you
Away, I'm bound away, 'cross the wide Missouri.

—traditional

In Mammoth Cave

No part of Mammoth Cave was to me more impressive than its entrance, probably because here its gigantic proportions are first revealed to you, and can be clearly seen. That strange colossal underworld here looks out into the light of day, and comes in contrast with familiar scenes and objects. When you are fairly in the cave, you cannot see it; that is, with your aboveground eyes; you walk along by the dim light of your lamp as in a huge wood at night; when the guide lights up the more interesting portions with his torches and colored lights, the effect is weird and spectral; it seems like a dream; it is an unfamiliar world; you hardly know whether this is the emotion of grandeur which you experience, or of mere strangeness. If you could have the light of day in there, you would come to your senses, and could test the reality of your impressions. At the entrance you have the light of day, and you look fairly in the face of this underground monster, yea, into his open mouth, which has a span of fifty feet or more, and down into his contracting throat, where a man can barely stand upright, and where the light fades and darkness begins . . . You see no sign of the cave till you emerge into a small opening where the grass grows and the sunshine falls, where you turn slightly to the right, and there at your feet yawns this terrible pit; and you feel indeed as if the mountain had opened its mouth and was lying in wait to swallow you down, as a whale might swallow a shrimp. I never grew tired of sitting or standing here by this entrance and gazing into it.

—John Burroughs
essayist and environmentalist

from *Journey*

The world is mine: blue hill, still silver lake,
Broad field, bright flower, and the long white road
A gateless garden, and an open path:
My feet to follow, and my heart to hold.

—Edna St. Vincent Millay
poet

from *The Lake Isle of Innisfree*

I will arise and go now, for always night and day
I hear lake water lapping with low sounds by the shore;
While I stand on the roadway, or on the pavements gray,
I hear it in the deep heart's core.

—William Butler Yeats
poet

In
Wildness
is the
preservation
of
the world.

—HENRY DAVID THOREAU
WRITER AND ENVIRONMENTALIST

Service

The greatest virtues are those which are most useful to other persons.

**—Aristotle
philosopher**

The Right Reward

It was a hot and dusty July afternoon when two Boy Scouts were completing their fourteen-mile hike for their First Class Badge.

All of a sudden they came upon a lady's purse, half-buried in the dust, at the edge of the trail. They discovered that it contained $20 in cash, and a card that stated the owner's lodge reservation for the current week expired at 8:00 a.m. the next day. They realized that in order to return the purse to the owner, it would mean hiking back up the trail for five miles. This extra time would consume their chances of swimming and perhaps also their chances of having a good supper. Yes, it also meant ten additional miles of hiking for

two already tired boys. Some might have been tempted to take the $20, discard the purse, and go to camp. But these boys were different.

They turned around and hiked as fast as they could back to the lodge. Upon inquiring for the owner of the purse, Mrs. Smith, the two boys were informed by the lodge manager that she was out horseback riding and would not return for one hour. The boys presented the manager with the purse and commenced to hike back to camp. The manager called after them, requesting their names. The boys shouted back, "Oh, we are just a couple of Boy Scouts!"

The next morning on her way back to the city, Mrs. Smith stopped at the Boy Scout Camp, and requested to see the boys that had returned her purse. Immediately, a camp assembly was called, which every Scoutmaster and boy promptly answered. The Camp Director introduced Mrs. Smith, relating her request to them, but there was no answer. Unnoticed in the line-up were two boys grinning at each other. Then Mrs. Smith asked the Camp Director to accept a reward to present to the boys when their identity became known. He refused to accept the gift, informing Mrs. Smith that Boy Scouts never accept pay for their good turns. Upon departing, Mrs. Smith thanked the Camp Director, saying, "I had not realized before that there was such a boy's program as this to build the characters of boys. Thank you again."

It is experiences such as this that make Scouting worthwhile.

—Kenneth Cheeseman
writer

Light of the World

Ye are the light of the world. A city that is set on an hill cannot be hid. Neither do men light a candle, and put it under a bushel, but on a candlestick; and it giveth light unto all that are in the house.

Let your light so shine before men, that they may see your good works, and glorify your Father which is in heaven.

—Matthew 5:14-16

So long as we love, we serve.

—Robert Louis Stevenson
author of *Treasure Island*

In the arena of human life the honors and rewards fall to those who show their good qualities in action.

—Aristotle
philosopher

43

Everybody can
be great.
Because anybody
can serve. . . .
You only need
a heart full of grace.
A soul generated
by love.

—MARTIN LUTHER KING JR.
ACTIVIST AND
NOBEL PRIZE LAUREATE

The Beggar Man

I was passing along the street when a beggar, a decrepit old man, stopped me. Swollen, tearful eyes, blue lips, bristling rags, unclean sores . . . Oh, how horribly had poverty gnawed that unhappy being!

He stretched out to me a red, bloated, dirty hand. He moaned, bellowed for help. I began to rummage in all my pockets. Neither purse, nor watch, nor even handkerchief did I find . . . I had taken nothing with me.

And the beggar still waited and extended his hand, which swayed and trembled feebly. Bewildered, confused, I shook that dirty, tremulous hand heartily.

"Blame me not, brother," I said. "I have nothing, brother."

The beggar man fixed his swollen eyes upon me; his blue lips smiled—and in his turn he pressed my cold fingers.

"Never mind, brother," he mumbled. "Thanks for this also, brother. This also is an alms, brother."

I understood that I had received an alms from my brother.

**—Ivan Turgenev
novelist and playwright**

The place to be happy is here. The time to be happy is now. The way to be happy is to make others so.

**—Robert G. Ingersoll
politician and public speaker**

God, Country, and Self

The American's Creed

I believe in the United States of America as a government of the people, by the people, for the people; whose just powers are derived from the consent of the governed; a democracy in a republic and a sovereign nation of many sovereign states; a perfect union, one and inseparable; established upon those principles of freedom, equality, justice, and humanity for which American patriots sacrificed their lives and fortunes.

I, therefore, believe it is my duty to my country to love it, to support its Constitution, to obey its laws, to respect its flag and to defend it against all enemies.

—William Tyler Page
author and public servant

from *Self-Reliance*

Insist on yourself; never imitate. Your own gift you can present every moment with the cumulative force of a whole life's cultivation; but of the adopted talent of another, you have only an extemporaneous, half possession. That which each can do best, none but his Maker can teach him. No man yet knows what it is, nor can, till that person has exhibited it.

SCOTLAND

Everything that I have written, every greatness that has been in any thought of mine, whatever I have done in my life has simply been due to the fact that when I was a child my mother daily read with me a part of the Bible and made me learn a part of it by heart.

—JOHN RUSKIN
WRITER AND ARTIST

Where is the master who could have taught Shakespeare?
. . . Dwell up there in the simple and noble regions of thy
life, obey thy heart, and thou shalt reproduce the Foreworld
again.

—Ralph Waldo Emerson
philosopher, poet, and essayist

I Hear America Singing

I hear America singing, the varied carols I hear,
Those of mechanics, each one singing is as it should be
      blithe and strong,
The carpenter singing his as he measures his plank or beam,
The mason singing his as he makes ready for work, or leaves
      off work,
The boatman singing what belongs to him in his boat, the
      deck-hand singing on the steamboat deck,
The shoemaker singing as he sits on his bench, the hatter
      singing as he stands,
The wood-cutter's song, the plowboy's on his way in the
      morning, or at noon intermission or at sundown,
The delicious singing of the mother, or of the young wife at
      work, or of the girl sewing or washing,
Each singing what belongs to him or her and to none else,
The day what belongs to the day—at night the party of
      young fellows, robust, friendly,
Singing with their open mouths and their strong melodious
      voices.

—Walt Whitman
poet

I decline to accept the end of man. It is easy enough to say that man is immortal simply because he will endure: that when the last ding-dong of doom has clanged and faded from the last worthless rock hanging tideless in the last red and dying evening, that even then there will be one more sound: that of his puny inexhaustible voice, still talking. I refuse to accept this. I believe that man will not merely endure: he will prevail. He is immortal, not because he alone among creatures has an inexhaustible voice, but because he has a soul, a spirit capable of compassion and sacrifice and endurance.

—William Faulkner
writer and Nobel Prize laureate

In Flanders Fields
In Flanders fields the poppies blow
Between the crosses, row on row,
    That mark our place; and in the sky
    The larks, still bravely singing, fly
Scarce heard amid the guns below.

A man's country
is not a certain area
of land, of mountains,
rivers, and woods,
but it is a principle;
and patriotism is
loyalty to that principle.

—GEORGE WILLIAM CURTIS
WRITER AND PUBLIC SPEAKER

We are the Dead. Short days ago
We lived, felt dawn, saw sunset glow,
    Loved and were loved, and now we lie
    In Flanders fields.

Take up our quarrel with the foe:
To you from failing hands we throw
    The torch; be yours to hold it high.
    If ye break faith with us who die
We shall not sleep, though poppies grow
    In Flanders fields.

**—John McCrae
soldier, physician, and poet**

I Never Saw a Moor

I never saw a moor,
I never saw the sea;
Yet know I how the heather looks,
And what a wave must be.

I never spoke with God,
Nor visited in heaven;
Yet certain am I of the spot
As if the chart were given.

**—Emily Dickinson
poet**

America

My country, 'tis of thee,
Sweet land of liberty, of thee I sing;
Land where my fathers died
Land of the pilgrims' pride
From every mountainside
Let freedom ring!

My native country, thee,
Land of the noble free,
Thy name I love;
I love thy rocks and rills,
Thy woods and templed hills;
My heart with rapture thrills
Like that above.

Let music swell the breeze,
And ring from all the trees
Sweet freedom's song;
Let mortal tongues awake;
Let all that breathe partake;
Let rocks their silence break,
The sound prolong.

Our father's God to Thee,
Author of liberty,
To Thee we sing.
Long may our land be bright,
With freedom's holy light,
Protect us with Thy might,
Great God our King.

—Samuel Smith
reverend

America the Beautiful

O beautiful for spacious skies,
For amber waves of grain,
For purple mountain majesties
Above the fruited plain!
America! America!
God shed his grace on thee
And crown thy good with brotherhood
From sea to shining sea!

O beautiful for Pilgrim feet,
Whose stern, impassioned stress
A thoroughfare for freedom beat
Across the wilderness!
America! America!
God mend thine every flaw,
Confirm thy soul in self-control,
Thy liberty in law!

O beautiful for heroes proved
In liberating strife,
Who more than self their country
   loved,
And mercy more than life!
America! America!
May God thy gold refine,
Till all success be nobleness
And every grain divine!

O beautiful for patriot dream
That sees beyond the years
Thine alabaster cities gleam
Undimmed by human tears!
America! America!
God shed His grace on thee,
And crown thy good with brotherhood
From sea to shining sea!

—KATHARINE LEE BATES
AUTHOR AND TEACHER

Truth Never Dies

Truth never dies. The ages come and go.
The mountains wear away, the stars retire.
Destruction lays earth's mighty cities low;
    And empires, states and dynasties expire;
But caught and handed onward by the wise,
    Truth never dies.

Though unreceived and scoffed at through the years;
    Though made the butt of ridicule and jest;
Though held aloft for mockery and jeers,
    Denied by those of transient power possessed,
Insulted by the insolence of lies,
    Truth never dies.

It answers not. It does not take offense,
    But with a mighty silence bides its time;
As some great cliff that braves the elements
    And lifts through all the storms its head sublime,
It ever stands, uplifted by the wise;
    And never dies.

As rests the Sphinx amid Egyptian sands;
    As looms on high the snowy peak and crest;
As firm and patient as Gibraltar stands,
    So truth, unwearied, waits the era blessed
When men shall turn to it with great surprise.
    Truth never dies.

—Anonymous

Defence of Fort McHenry

O! say can you see, by the dawn's early light,
 What so proudly we hail'd at the twilight's last gleaming,
Whose broad stripes and bright stars through the perilous
  fight,
 O'er the ramparts we watched, were so gallantly
  streaming?
  And the rockets' red glare, the bombs bursting in air,
  Gave proof through the night that our flag was still
   there—
   O! say does that star-spangled banner yet wave
   O'er the land of the free and the home of the brave?

On the shore, dimly seen through the mists of the deep,
 Where the foes haughty host in dread silence reposes,
What is that which the breeze o'er the towering steep,
 As it fitfully blows, half conceals, half discloses?
  Now it catches the gleam of the morning's first beam,
  In full glory reflected now shines on the stream—
   'Tis the star-spangled banner, O! long may it wave
   O'er the land of the free, and the home of the brave.

And where is that band who so vauntingly swore
 That the havock of war and the battle's confusion
A home and a country should leave us no more?
 Their blood has wash'd out their foul foot-steps' pollution.
  No refuge could save the hireling and slave,
  From the terror of flight or the gloom of the grave;
   And the star-spangled banner in triumph doth wave
   O'er the land of the free and the home of the brave.

I have a dream that one day every valley shall be exalted, every hill and mountain shall be made low, the rough places will be made plain, and the crooked places will be made straight, and the glory of the Lord shall be revealed, and all flesh will see it together.

—MARTIN LUTHER KING JR.
ACTIVIST AND
NOBEL PRIZE LAUREATE

O! thus be it ever when freemen shall stand
  Between their lov'd home, and the war's desolation,
Blest with vict'ry and peace, may the heav'n-rescued land
  Praise the power that hath made and preserv'd us a
      nation!
  Then conquer we must, when our cause it is just,
  And this be our motto—"In God is our trust!"
    And the star-spangled banner in triumph shall wave
    O'er the land of the free and the home of the brave.

**—Francis Scott Key
lawyer and writer**

Prayer for Americans

God of the free, we pledge our hearts and lives today to the cause of all free mankind.

Grant us victory over the tyrants who would enslave all free men and nations. Grant us faith and understanding to cherish all those who fight for freedom as if they were our brothers. Grant us brotherhood in hope and union, not only for the space of this bitter war, but for the days to come which shall and must unite all the children of the earth.

Our earth is but a small star in the great universe. Yet of it we can make, if we choose, a planet unvexed by war, undivided by senseless distinctions of race, color, or theory. Grant us that courage and foreseeing to begin this task today that our children and our children's children may be proud of the name of man.

The spirit of man has awakened and the soul of man has gone forth. Grant us the wisdom and the vision to comprehend

59

the greatness of man's spirit, that suffers and endures so hugely for a goal beyond his own brief span. Grant us honor for our dead who died in the faith, honor for our living who work and strive for the faith, redemption and security for all the captive lands and peoples. Grant us patience with the deluded and pity for the betrayed. And grant us the skill and the valor that shall cleanse the world of oppression and the old base doctrine that the strong must eat the weak because they are strong.

Yet most of all grant us brotherhood, not only for this day but for all our years—a brotherhood, not of words but of acts and deeds. We are all of us children of earth—grant us that simple knowledge. If our brothers are oppressed, then we are oppressed. If they hunger, we hunger. If their freedom is taken away, our freedom is not secure.

Grant us a common faith that man shall know bread and peace—that he shall know justice and righteousness, freedom and security, and equal opportunity and an equal chance to do his best, not only in our lands but throughout the world. And in that faith let us march toward the clean world our hands can make. Amen.

—Steven Vincent Benét
poet and novelist

Far away there in the sunshine are my highest aspirations. I may not reach them, but I can look up and see their beauty, believe in them, and try to follow where they lead.

—Louisa May Alcott
writer

All the world cries, "Where is the man who will save us? We want a man!" Don't look so far for this man. You have him at hand. This man—it is you, it is I, it is each one of us!

—ALEXANDRE DUMAS
AUTHOR OF
THE THREE MUSKETEERS

Trustworthiness

Whoever can be trusted with very little can also be trusted with much, and whoever is dishonest with very little also will be dishonest with much.

—Luke 16:10

All truth is safe and nothing else is safe; and he who keeps back the truth, or withholds it from men, from motives of expediency, is either a coward or a criminal, or both.

—Max Müller
philosopher

An honest man's the noblest work of God.

—Alexander Pope
poet

I would
prefer
even to fail
with honor
than to win
by
cheating.

—SOPHOCLES
PLAYWRIGHT

ATERIAL FOR A GOOD Y

A man who doesn't trust himself can never really trust anyone else.

—Cardinal de Retz
clergyman and writer

Honesty is the first chapter in the book of wisdom.

—Thomas Jefferson
former United States president

Always do right. This will gratify some people and astonish the rest.

—Mark Twain
writer and humorist

This above all: To thine own self be true, and it must follow, as the night the day, thou canst not then be false to any man.

—William Shakespeare
poet and playwright

Be true to your work, your word, and your friend.

—Henry David Thoreau
writer and environmentalist

I hope I shall always have firmness and virtue enough to maintain what I consider the most enviable of all titles, the character of an honest man.

—George Washington
former United States president

It
does not
require
many words
to
speak
the truth.

—CHIEF JOSEPH
NEZ PERCE LEADER

Loyalty

Loyalty is a feature in a boy's character that inspires boundless hope.

**—Robert Baden-Powell
co-founder of the Boy Scouts of America**

The Story of Castor and Pollux

Among the constellations in the sky may be found the one called Gemini, or the Twins. The ancient Greeks used to believe that twin brothers named Castor and Pollux had been really placed in the sky. They once lived in Sparta; their mother was the lovely Leda, and one of their sisters was the beautiful Helen, whose capture caused the famous Trojan War.

These brothers were as devoted to each other as twins are said to be, and one was never seen without the other being near. Their love for their sisters was very great, and once when Helen was captured by two noted warriors, these twin brothers of hers found her and brought her safely back to their mother's house.

Castor was very fond of horses. He could tame the wildest one that was ever caught, and lead it about like a pet dog as soon as his magic touch had taught its fiery spirit that he was its master. He could ride better than anyone in the kingdom, for no horse had ever thrown him.

Loyalty is that quality which prompts a person to be true to the thing he understands. It means definite direction, fixity of purpose.

—ELBERT HUBBARD
WRITER AND PHILOSOPHER

Pollux was just as famous in boxing and wrestling. He taught young men many tricks with the hand and foot, and was the leader in all games.

The two brothers were proud to be allowed to go with the other heroes in quest of the golden fleece. When the sweet music of Orpheus stilled the wild storm that arose on the sea and threatened to wreck the Argo, stars appeared upon the heads of Castor and Pollux, for their great love for each other was known to the Olympian gods who had sent the storm.

When the curious flames, that sometimes during storms play about the masts and sails of a ship, were seen on other ships after this voyage of the Argo, the sailors would always cry out, "See the stars of Castor and Pollux!"

Their love for each other made them more famous than anything else. When at last Castor was slain in a great battle, Pollux prayed to Jupiter to let them again be united. The prayer was granted. Not long after this, the poets tell us, the constellation of the Twins was discovered in the sky, and there the two loving brothers stay forever watching the earth to see if they may help others to be faithful to the end.

—Retold by Mary Catherine Judd
school principal and writer

To all you serve, be loyal.

—Confucius
philosopher and educator

Loyalty means nothing unless it has at its heart the absolute principle of self-sacrifice.

—Woodrow Wilson
former United States president

Helpfulness

The Good Samaritan

A certain man went down from Jerusalem to Jericho, and fell among thieves, which stripped him of his raiment, and wounded him, and departed, leaving him half dead.

And by chance there came down a certain priest that way: and when he saw him, he passed on the other side.

And likewise a Levite, when he was at the place, came and looked on him, and passed on the other side.

But a certain Samaritan, as he journeyed, came where he was: and when he saw him, he had compassion on him, and went to him, and bound up his wounds, pouring in oil and wine, and set him on his own beast, and brought him to an inn, and took care of him.

And on the morrow when he departed, he took out two pence, and gave them to the host, and said unto him, Take care of him; and whatsoever thou spendest more, when I come again, I will repay thee.

Which now of these three thinkest thou, was neighbor unto him that fell among the thieves?

And he said, He that shewed mercy on him. Then said Jesus unto him, Go, and do thou likewise.

—Luke 10:30-37

You must
be the
change
you wish
to see
in the
world.

—MAHATMA GANDHI
WRITER, ACTIVIST, AND
SPIRITUAL LEADER

Today is your day and mine, the only day we have, the day in which we play our part. What our part may signify in the great whole we may not understand; but we are here to play it, and now is our time. This we know: it is a part of action, not of whining. It is a part of love, not cynicism. It is for us to express love in terms of human helpfulness.

—David Starr Jordan
teacher

When men are rightly occupied, their amusement grows out of their work, as the color petals out of a fruitful flower; when they are faithfully helpful and compassionate, all their emotions are steady, deep, perpetual, and vivifying to the soul as is the natural pulse to the body.

—John Ruskin
writer and artist

Down in their hearts, wise men know this truth: The only way to help yourself is to help others.

—Elbert Hubbard
writer and philosopher

The Toilers

Here's to the man who labors and does it with a song!
He stimulates his neighbors and helps the world along.
I like the men who do things, who hustle and achieve;
    the men who saw and glue things, and spin and dig and
        weave.
Man groans beneath his burden, beneath the chain he wears;
    and still the toiler's guerdon is worth the pain he bears.
For there is no satisfaction beneath the bending sky
    like that the man of action enjoys when night is nigh.
To look back o'er the winding and dark and rocky road,
    and know you bore your grinding and soul-fatiguing
        load,
As strong men ought to bear it, through all the stress and
        strife—
    that's the reward of merit—that is the balm of life.
I like the men who do things, who plow and sow and reap,
    who build and delve and hew things while the dreamers
        are asleep.

—Walt Mason
writer and poet

7 6

The
path
of the
lazy
leads to
disgrace.

—OMAHA INDIAN PROVERB

Go Forth to Life

Go forth to life, oh! child of Earth.
Still mindful of thy heavenly birth;
Thou art not here for ease or sin,
But manhood's noble crown to win.

Though passion's fires are in thy soul,
Thy spirit can thy flames control;
Though tempters strong beset thy way,
Thy spirit is more strong than they.

Go on from innocence of youth
To manly pureness, manly truth;
God's angels still are near to save,
And God himself doth help the brave.

Then forth to life, oh! child of Earth,
Be worthy of thy heavenly birth,
For noble service thou art here;
Thy brothers help, thy God revere!

**—Samuel Longfellow
clergyman and hymn writer**

The duty of helping the helpless is one that speaks trumpet-tongued; but especially to those who profess to love God and goodwill to men. It is a duty that belongs to men as individuals, and as members of the social body. As individuals, because we are enjoined to help the widow and the fatherless in their affliction; and as members of the social body, because society claims of every man that he shall be a helper in the cause of progress and of social well-being.

—Samuel Smiles
writer

No man is an island entire of itself; every man is a piece of the continent, a part of the main.

—John Donne
poet and clergyman

Don't waste yourself in rejection, nor bark against the bad, but chant the beauty of the good.

—Ralph Waldo Emerson
philosopher, poet, and essayist

Friendliness

The Touch of a Hand

It's the human touch in this world that counts
The touch of your hand and mine
That means far more to the fainting heart
Than shelter or bread or wine
For shelter is gone when the night is o'er
And bread lasts only a day
But the touch of a hand and the sound of a voice
Sing on in the soul always.

—Anonymous

Friendship

If a friend of mine—gave a feast, and did not invite me to it, I should not mind a bit . . . but if . . . a friend of mine had a sorrow and refused to allow me to share it, I should feel it most bitterly. If he shut the doors of the house of mourning against me, I would move back again and again and beg to be admitted, so that I might share in what I was entitled to share. If he thought me unworthy, unfit to weep with him, I should feel it as the most poignant humiliation, as the most

terrible moment for which disgrace could be inflicted on me
... he who can look on the loveliness of the world and share
its sorrow, and realize something of the wonder of both, is in
immediate contact with divine things, and has got as near to
God's secret as anyone can get.

—Oscar Wilde
writer and poet

from
The House by the Side of the Road
I see from my house by the side of the road,
    By the side of the highway of life,
The men who press with the ardor of hope,
    The men who are faint with the strife.
But I turn not away from their smiles nor their tears—
    Both parts of an infinite plan;
Let me live in my house by the side of the road
And be a friend to man.

—Sam Walter Foss
poet and librarian

Damon and Pythias
Damon and Pythias had been the best of friends since child-
hood. Each trusted the other like a brother, and each knew in
his heart there was nothing he would not do for his friend.
Eventually the time came for them to prove the depth of their

Happy is
the house
that
shelters
a friend!

—RALPH WALDO EMERSON
PHILOSOPHER, POET, AND ESSAYIST

devotion. It happened this way:

Dionysius, the ruler of Syracuse, grew annoyed when he heard about the kind of speeches Pythias was giving. The young scholar was telling the public that no man should have unlimited power over another, and that absolute tyrants were unjust kings. In a fit of rage, Dionysius summoned Pythias and his friend.

"Who do you think you are, spreading unrest among the people?" he demanded.

"I spread only the truth," Pythias answered. "There can be nothing wrong with that."

"And does your truth hold that kings have too much power and that their laws are not good for their subjects?"

"If a king has seized power without permission of the people, then that is what I say."

"This kind of talk is treason," Dionysius shouted. "You are conspiring to overthrow me. Retract what you've said, or face the consequences."

"I will retract nothing," Pythias answered.

"Then you will die. Do you have any last requests?"

"Yes. Let me go home just long enough to say goodbye to my wife and children and to put my household in order."

"I see you not only think I'm unjust, you think I'm stupid as well," Dionysius laughed scornfully. "If I let you leave Syracuse, I have no doubt I will never see you again."

"I will give you a pledge," Pythias said.

"What kind of pledge could you possibly give to make me think you will ever return?" Dionysius demanded.

At that instant, Damon, who had stood quietly beside his friend, stepped forward.

"I will be his pledge," he said. "Keep me here in Syracuse, as your prisoner, until Pythias returns. Our friendship is well known to you. You can be sure Pythias will return so long as you hold me."

Dionysius studied the two friends silently. "Very well," he

said at last. "But if you are willing to take the place of your friend, you must be willing to accept his sentence if he breaks his promise. If Pythias does not return to Syracuse, you will die in his place."

"He will keep his word," Damon replied. "I have no doubt of that."

Pythias was allowed to go free for a time, and Damon was thrown into prison. After several days, when Pythias failed to reappear, Dionysius's curiosity got the better of him, and he went to the prison to see if Damon was sorry he had made such a bargain.

"Your time is almost up," the ruler of Syracuse sneered. "It will be useless to beg for mercy. You were a fool to rely on your friend's promise. Did you really think he would sacrifice his life for you or anyone else?"

"He has merely been delayed," Damon answered steadily. "The winds have kept him from sailing, or perhaps he has met with some accident on the road. But if it is humanly possible, he will be here on time. I am as confident of his virtue as I am of my own existence."

Dionysius was startled at the prisoner's confidence. "We shall soon see," he said, and left Damon in his cell.

The fatal day arrived. Damon was brought from prison and led before the executioner. Dionysius greeted him with a smug smile.

"It seems your friend has not turned up," he laughed. "What do you think of him now?"

"He is my friend," Damon answered. "I trust him."

Even as he spoke, the doors flew open, and Pythias staggered into the room. He was pale and bruised and half speechless from exhaustion. He rushed to the arms of his friend.

"You are safe, praise the gods," he gasped. "It seemed as though the fates were conspiring against us. My ship was wrecked in a storm, and then bandits attacked me on the road. But I refused to give up hope, and at last I've made it back in time. I am ready to receive my sentence of death."

Dionysius heard his words with astonishment. His eyes and his heart were opened. It was impossible for him to resist the power of such constancy.

"The sentence is revoked," he declared. "I never believed that such faith and loyalty could exist in friendship. You have shown me how wrong I was, and it is only right that you be rewarded with your freedom. But I ask in return you do me one great service."

"What service do you mean?" the friends asked.

"Teach me how to be part of so worthy a friendship."

—Adapted from Thomas Bulfinch
writer and editor

A blessed thing it is for any man or woman to have a friend, one human soul whom we can trust utterly, who knows the best and worst of us, and who loves us in spite of all our faults.

—Charles Kingsley
clergyman and novelist

The
only way
to have
a friend
is to
be one.

—RALPH WALDO EMERSON
PHILOSOPHER, POET, AND ESSAYIST

Don't wait
for people
to be
friendly,
show
them
how.

—ANONYMOUS

Life is to be fortified by many friendships. To love and to be loved is the greatest happiness of existence.

—Sydney Smith
writer and clergyman

Too often we underestimate the power of a touch, a smile, a kind word, a listening ear, an honest compliment, or the smallest act of caring, all of which have the potential to turn a life around.

—Leo Buscaglia
writer and motivational speaker

If someone listens, or stretches out a hand, or whispers a kind word of encouragement, or attempts to understand a lonely person, extraordinary things begin to happen.

—Loretta Girzartis
writer

Courteousness

A man asked to define the essential characteristics of a gentleman—using the term in its widest sense—would presumably reply, "The will to put himself in the place of others; the horror of forcing others into positions from which he would himself recoil; the power to do what seems to him to be right, without considering what others may say or think.

—John Galsworthy
writer and Nobel Prize laureate

If a man be gracious and courteous to strangers, it shows he is a citizen of the world, and that his heart is no island cut off from other lands, but a continent that joins them.

—Francis Bacon
essayist and philosopher

Courtesy
is as
much
a mark
of a
gentleman
as courage.

—THEODORE ROOSEVELT
FORMER UNITED STATES
PRESIDENT

The greater man the greater courtesy.

—Lord Alfred Tennyson
poet

We are what we repeatedly do.

—Aristotle
philosopher

All doors open to courtesy.

—Thomas Fuller
clergyman and writer

Kindness

Be kind, for everyone you meet is fighting a hard battle.

—Plato
philosopher

Androcles and the Lion

In Rome there was once a poor slave whose name was Androcles. His master was a cruel man, and so unkind to him that at last Androcles ran away.

He hid himself in a wood for many days. But there was no food to be found, and he grew so weak and sick that he thought he would die. So one day he crept into a cave and lay down, and soon he was fast asleep.

After a while a great noise woke him up. A lion had come into the cave, and was roaring loudly. Androcles was very much afraid, for he felt sure that the beast would kill him. Soon, however, he saw that the lion was not angry, but that he limped as though his foot hurt him.

Then Androcles grew so bold that he took hold of the lion's lame paw to see what was the matter. The lion stood quite still, and rubbed his head against the man's shoulder.

He seemed to say, "I know that you will help me."

Androcles lifted the paw from the ground, and saw that it was a long, sharp thorn which hurt the lion so much. He took the end of the thorn in his fingers; then he gave a strong, quick pull, and out it came. The lion was full of joy. He jumped about like a dog, and licked the hands and feet of his new friend.

Androcles was not at all afraid after this. And when night came, he and the lion lay down and slept side by side.

For a long time, the lion brought food to Androcles every day, and the two became such good friends that Androcles found his new life a very happy one.

One day some soldiers who were passing through the wood found Androcles in the cave. They knew who he was, and so took him back to Rome.

It was the law at that time that every slave who ran away from his master should be made to fight a hungry lion. So a fierce lion was shut up for a while without food, and a time was set for the fight.

When the day came, thousands of people crowded to see the sport. They went to such places at that time very much as people now go to the circus show, or a game of baseball.

The door opened, and poor Androcles was brought in. He was almost dead with fear, for the roars of the lion could already be heard. He looked up, and saw that there was no pity in the thousands of faces around him.

Then the hungry lion rushed in. With a single bound he reached the poor slave. Androcles gave a great cry, not of fear, but of gladness. It was his old friend, the lion of the cave.

The people, who had expected to see the man killed by the lion, were filled with wonder. They saw Androcles put his arms around the lion's neck; they saw the lion lie down at his feet, and lick them lovingly; they saw the great beast rub his head against the slave's face as though he wanted to be petted. They could not understand what it all meant.

After a while they asked Androcles to tell them about it. So he stood up before them, and, with his arm around the lion's neck, told how he and the beast had lived together in the cave.

"I am a man," he said, "but no man has ever befriended me. This poor lion alone has been kind to me and we love each other as brothers."

The people were not so bad that they could be cruel to the poor slave now. "Live and be free!" they cried. "Live and be free!"

Others cried, "Let the lion go free too! Give both of them their liberty!"

And so Androcles was set free, and the lion was given to him for his own. And they lived together in Rome for many years.

—Retold by James Baldwin
writer and essayist

No act of kindness, no matter how small, is ever wasted.

—Aesop
Greek storyteller

Wherever there is a human being, there is an opportunity for kindness.

—Lucius Annaeus Seneca the Elder
philosopher and dramatist

I can
live
for two
months
on a
good
compliment.

—MARK TWAIN
WRITER AND HUMORIST

No kind action ever stops with itself. One kind action leads to another.

—Amelia Earhart
aviation pioneer and writer

If I Can Stop One Heart from Breaking

If I can stop one heart from breaking,
I shall not live in vain;
If I can ease one life the aching,
Or cool one pain,
Or help one fainting robin
Unto his nest again,
I shall not live in vain.

—Emily Dickinson
poet

Kind words do not cost much. Yet they accomplish much.

—Blaise Pascal
mathematician and philosopher

Obedience

You cannot escape the responsibility of tomorrow by evading it today.

**—Abraham Lincoln
former United States president**

Icarus and Daedalus

Daedalus was the most skillful builder and inventor of his day in ancient Greece. He built magnificent palaces and gardens, and created wonderful works of art throughout the land. His statues were so beautifully crafted they were taken for living beings, and it was believed they could see and walk about. People said someone as cunning as Daedalus must have learned the secrets of his craft from the gods themselves.

Now across the sea, on the island of Crete, lived a king named Minos. King Minos had a terrible monster that was half bull and half man called the Minotaur, and he needed someplace to keep it. When he heard of Daedalus's cleverness, he invited him to come to his country and build a prison to hold the beast. So Daedalus and his young son, Icarus, sailed to Crete, and there Daedalus built the famous Labyrinth, a

True
obedience
is
true
liberty.

—HENRY WARD BEECHER
CLERGYMAN AND ACTIVIST

maze of winding passages so tangled and twisted that whoever went in could never find their way out. And there they put the Minotaur.

When the Labyrinth was finished, Daedalus wanted to sail back to Greece with his son, but Minos had made up his mind to keep them in Crete. He wanted Daedalus to stay and invent more wonderful devices for him, so he locked them both in a high tower beside the sea. The king knew Daedalus was clever enough to escape from the tower, so he also ordered that every ship in Crete be searched for stowaways before sailing away from Crete.

Other men may have given up, but not Daedalus. From his high tower he watched the seagulls drifting on the ocean breezes. "Minos may control the land and sea," he said, "but he does not rule the air. We'll go that way."

So he summoned all the secrets of his craft, and he set to work. Little by little, he gathered a great pile of feathers of all sizes. He fastened them together with thread, and molded them with wax, and at last he had two great wings like those of the seagulls. He tied them to his shoulders, and after one or two clumsy efforts, he found that by waving his arms he could rise into the air. He held himself aloft, wavering this way and that with the wind, until he taught himself how to glide and soar on the currents as gracefully as any gull.

Next he built a second pair of wings for Icarus. He taught the boy how to move the feathers and rise a few feet into the air, and then let him fly back and forth across the room. Then he taught him how to ride the air currents, climbing in circles, and hang in the winds. They practiced together until Icarus was ready.

Finally the day came when the winds were just right. Father and son strapped on their wings and prepared to fly home.

"Remember all I've told you," Daedalus said. "Above all, remember you must not fly too high or too low. If you fly too

103

low, the ocean sprays will clog your wings and make them too heavy. If you fly too high, the heat of the sun will melt the wax, and your wings will fall apart. Stay close to me, and you'll be fine."

Up they rose, the boy after his father, and the hateful ground of Crete sank far beneath them. As they flew the plowman stopped his work to gaze, and the shepherd leaned on his staff to watch them, and people came running out of their houses to catch a glimpse of the two figures high above the treetops. Surely they were gods—Apollo, perhaps, with Cupid after him.

At first the flight seemed terrible to both Daedalus and Icarus. The wide, endless sky dazed them, and even the quickest glance down made their brains reel. But gradually they grew used to riding among the clouds, and they lost their fear. Icarus felt the wind fill his wings and lift him higher and higher, and began to sense a freedom he had never known before. He looked down with great excitement at all the islands they passed, and their people, and at the broad blue sea spread out beneath him, dotted with the white sails of ships. He soared higher and higher, forgetting his father's warning. He forgot everything in the world but joy.

"Come back!" Daedalus called frantically. "You're flying too high! Remember the sun! Come down! Come down!"

But Icarus thought of nothing but his own excitement and glory. He longed to fly as close as he could to the heavens. Nearer and nearer he came to the sun, and slowly his wings began to soften. One by one the feathers began to fall and scatter in the air, and suddenly the wax melted all at once. Icarus felt himself falling. He fluttered his arms as fast as he could, but no feathers remained to hold the air. He cried out for his father, but it was too late—with a scream he fell from his lofty height and plunged into the sea, disappearing beneath the waves.

Daedalus circled over the water again and again, but he

saw nothing but feathers floating on the waves, and he knew his son was gone. At last the body came to the surface, and he managed to pluck it from the sea. With a heavy burden and broken heart Daedalus slowly flew away. When he reached land, he buried his son and built a temple to the gods. Then he hung up his wings, and he never flew again.

—Retold by Thomas Bulfinch
writer and editor

Give all to love; obey thy heart.

—Ralph Waldo Emerson
poet, philosopher, and essayist

Wicked men obey from fear; good men, from love.

—Aristotle
philosopher

Cheerfulness

Thank God every morning when you get up that you have something to do that day which must be done whether you like it or not. Being forced to work, and forced to do your best, will breed in you temperance and self-control, diligence and strength of will, cheerfulness and content, and a hundred virtues which the idle will never know.

—Charles Kingsley
clergyman and novelist

Life's Mirror
There are loyal hearts, there are spirits brave,
There are souls that are pure and true;
Then give to the world the best you have
And the best will come back to you.
Give love, and love to your life will flow,
A strength in your utmost need;
Have faith, and a score of hearts will show
Their faith in your word and deed.
Give truth, and your gift will be paid in kind,
And honor will honor meet

And a smile that is sweet will surely find
A smile that is just as sweet.
Give sorrow and pity to those who mourn
You will gather in flowers again
The scattered seeds of your thoughts outborne,
Though the sowing seem but vain.
For life is the mirror, of king and slave—
'Tis just what we are and do,
Then give to the world the best you have
And the best will come back to you.

—Mary Ainge de Vere
poet

The Arrow and the Song

I shot an arrow into the air,
It fell to earth, I know not where;
For, so swiftly it flew, the sight
Could not follow in its flight.
I breathed a song into the air,
It fell to earth, I know not where;
For who has sight so keen and strong
That it can follow the flight of a song?

Long, long afterward, in an oak
I found the arrow, still unbroke;
And the song from beginning to end,
I found again in the heart of a friend.

—Henry Wadsworth Longfellow
poet

No one has success until he has the abounding life. This is made up of the many-fold activity of energy, enthusiasm, and gladness. It is to spring to meet the day with a thrill at being alive. It is to go forth to meet the morning in an ecstasy of joy. It is to realize the oneness of humanity in true spiritual sympathy.

—Lilian Whiting
journalist and editor

I have told you of the man who always put on his spectacles to eat cherries, in order that the fruit might look larger and more tempting. In like manner I always make the most of my enjoyments, and, though I do not cast my eyes away from troubles, I pack them into as small a compass as I can for myself, and never let them annoy others.

—Robert Southey
poet

Cheerfulness, it would appear, is a matter which depends fully as much on the state of things within, as on the state of things without and around us

—Charlotte Brontë
novelist and poet

The best way
to cheer
yourself
is to try
to cheer
someone
else up.

—MARK TWAIN
WRITER AND HUMORIST

The most wasted of all days is that in which we have not laughed.

—Sebastien Chamfort
writer and playwright

Wondrous is the strength of cheerfulness, and its power of endurance—the cheerful man will do more in the same time, will do it better, will preserve it longer, than the sad or sullen.

—Thomas Carlyle
teacher and writer

I am still determined to be happy and cheerful in whatever situation I may be.

—Martha Washington
wife of George Washington

Thriftiness

Nowadays manual labor seems to be looked upon by everyone more in the light of a disgrace or punishment than as a privilege; nevertheless, it *is a privilege* to be able to labor, it *is a privilege* to have the vim, the pep, the desire and the ability to do things. Labor is a necessary attribute of the doer and those who live in the open; no one need attempt so simple a thing as the building of a fire and expect to succeed without labor.

—Daniel Carter Beard
co-founder of the Boy Scouts of America

Those who are to succeed must have the habit of thrift. The boy who, when he is fifteen years old . . . wastes neither his study-time nor his play-time, who already has a bank account, however small, who takes care of his health, is sure to succeed.

—Myron T. Prichard
school principal

Everyone is the son of his own work.

**—Miguel de Cervantes
writer**

Every Indian village in the old days had its granaries of corn, its stores of dried beans, berries, and pumpkin-strips, as well as its dried buffalo tongues, pemmican and deer's meat . . .

Many of the modern Indians, armed with rifles, have learned to emulate the white man, and slaughter game for the love of slaughter, without reference to the future. Such waste was condemned by the old-time Indians as an abuse of the gifts of God, and which would surely bring its punishment.

**—Ernest Thompson Seton
co-founder of the Boy Scouts of America**

It is thrifty to prepare today for the wants of tomorrow.

**—Aesop
storyteller**

It is not wealth that gives the true zest to life, but reflection, appreciation, taste, culture. Above all, the seeing eye and the feeling heart are indispensable. With these, the humblest lot may be made blest.

—Samuel Smiles
writer

Give me the money that has been spent in war, and I will clothe every man, woman, and child in an attire of which kings and queens would be proud. I will build a schoolhouse in every valley over the whole earth. I will crown every hillside with a place of worship consecrated to the gospel of peace.

—Charles Sumner
politician and public speaker

Among the aimless, unsuccessful, or worthless, you may often hear talk about "killing time." The man who is always killing time is really killing his own chances in life; while the man who is destined to success is the man who makes time live by making it useful.

—Arthur Brisbane
journalist and editor

Dost thou value life? Then guard well thy time, for time's the stuff life's made of.

—BENJAMIN FRANKLIN
POLITICIAN, WRITER, AND INVENTOR

Our life is frittered away by detail. Simplify, simplify.

—Henry David Thoreau
writer and environmentalist

It takes less time to do a thing right than it does to explain why you did it wrong.

—Henry Wadsworth Longfellow
poet

Thrift is not an affair of the pocket, but an affair of character.

—S. W. Straus
investment banker

The reward of a thing well done is to have done it.

—Ralph Waldo Emerson
philosopher, poet, and essayist

117

Bravery

When you get into a tight place and everything goes against you, till it seems as though you could not hold on a minute longer, never give up then, for that is just the place and time that the tide will turn.

—Harriet Beecher Stowe
author of *Uncle Tom's Cabin*

Great Men

Not gold, but only man can make
    A people great and strong;
Men who, for truth and honor's sake,
Stand fast and suffer long.

Brave men who work while others sleep,
    Who dare while others fly—
They build a nation's pillars deep
    And lift them to the sky.

—Ralph Waldo Emerson
philosopher, poet, and essayist

Courage
is resistance
to fear,
mastery of fear
—not
absence
of fear.

— MARK TWAIN
WRITER AND HUMORIST

Ulysses and the Cyclops

After defeating their enemies in the Trojan War, the wise king Ulysses and his men set sail to return to Greece and their families. But the sea god Poseidon was angry with Ulysses, and made him wander far and wide across the ocean before he was at last able to return home to his family. This is the story of how Ulysses defeated the formidable Cyclops—a giant with one eye set in the middle of his forehead:

Ulysses and his ships reached the coast of the land of the Cyclopes—the round-eyed men, with only one eye set in the middle of their foreheads. They lived in caves among the hills, and they had no king and no laws, and their only labor was tending great flocks of sheep.

Ulysses landed his ships on a beautiful desert island set in the mouth of a bay. The island was full of wild goats, and the men hunted and killed the goats and enjoyed a meal of fresh meat and wine. The next day, Ulysses took only his own ship and small crew to explore the mainland. There he discovered an enormous cave next to the sea, with laurels growing on the roof, and a wall of rough stones built around the front of the cave. Ulysses and twelve of his men took wine and corn flour from the ship and made their way to the cave. Nobody was there, but there were lambs scattered all about the mouth of the cave.

Everything seemed quiet and peaceful. Ulysses wanted to see if he could find out who was living in the cave, but his men went ahead and entered the cave to have a look around. Just then, a huge shadow filled the mouth of the cave, and a monstrous man entered, and threw down a dry trunk of a tree that he had carried in for firewood. Then he drove the sheep into the cave and picked up a gigantic stone and set it in front of the cave, so that nothing could come in or out.

At last the giant man lit a fire and happened to notice the men hiding in his cave.

"Who are you?" he asked. "And what are you doing here?"

121

"We are victorious soldiers returning from the Trojan War," said Ulysses. "We have been wandering the seas in search of our home."

"We Cyclopes," said the giant, "care little for the trivialities for men such as yourself. Where is your ship?"

Ulysses answered that his ship had been wrecked on the coast. The giant gave no answer, but quickly snatched up two of Ulysses' men, knocked their brains out on the floor, tore the bodies apart, roasted them over his fire, ate them, and then lay down and fell asleep.

The next morning, the giant ate two more of Ulysses' men for breakfast. Then he moved the giant stone from the mouth of his cave and drove the sheep out onto the open land.

Ulysses did not give in to despair. He noticed that the giant had left an enormous stick in the cave—it was as large as the mast of a ship. Ulysses took up the stick and cut away a portion six feet in length. Then he sharpened this portion to a point and hardened it in the fire. He and his men cast lots to determine who should twist the stick into the giant's eye after he fell asleep that night.

At sunset, the giant returned with his flock, and as he had done the night before, drove them into the cave and then set the huge stone in the mouth of the cave, so that nothing could come in or out.

Meanwhile, Ulysses had filled a wooden bowl with strong wine, which he offered to the giant, who had never tasted wine, or even heard of it. He drank many bowls until he was very tipsy, and he said that he would make Ulysses a present.

"What is your name?" the giant asked.

"My name is *Nobody*," said Ulysses.

"Then I shall eat the others first and Nobody last," said the giant. "That shall be your gift." Then he fell asleep.

Ulysses took up his stick of wood and made the point red-hot in the fire. Then four of his men rammed the stick into the giant's eye and held it down while Ulysses twisted it

If you do not want
to be forgotten
as soon as you are
dead and rotten,
either write things
worth reading, or
do things worth
the writing.

—BENJAMIN FRANKLIN
POLITICIAN, WRITER,
AND INVENTOR

The
greater
the obstacle,
the more
glory in
overcoming it.

— MOLIÈRE
PLAYWRIGHT AND ACTOR

around. The giant's eye hissed like a red-hot iron dipped into cold water. The Cyclops roared in pain and leapt to his feet and shouted for help to the other giants who lived nearby.

"Who is troubling you?" his neighbors asked. "Why did you wake us up?"

"*Nobody* is troubling me," said the giant.

"If nobody is troubling you," said the neighbors, "then nobody can help you. Now go back to sleep."

Realizing that he was not going to get any help from his neighbors, the giant crawled to the mouth of the cave and pulled away the huge stone. He wanted Ulysses and his men to try to escape, and when they did so, he would grab them and eat them up.

But Ulysses quickly put together a plan. He fastened three sheep together with twisted vines, and bound one of his men to the sheep in the middle, so that the now-blind giant would only feel the two outside sheep, and not the man hiding under the sheep in the middle. Then he did the same with the rest of his men, and with himself. All the sheep ran out through the cave entrance, and the giant felt them with his hands, but he did not notice Ulysses and his men hiding between the sheep.

The sheep ran out into the open country, and Ulysses unfastened himself and his men, and drove the sheep down onto his ship. Then Ulysses shouted back at the Cyclops, "If anyone asks who had blinded you, tell them it was I, Ulysses, the stormer of cities."

The giant picked up a huge rock and threw it in the direction of Ulysses' voice. The rock landed in the water near the ship, bringing up a large wave, but causing no damage to Ulysses or his men. The ship moved out to sea, and the giant fell to his knees in agony and defeat.

—Adapted from Thomas Bulfinch
writer and editor

By learning the sufferings and burdens of men, I became aware as never before of the life-power that has survived the forces of darkness—the power which, though never completely victorious, is continuously conquering. The very fact that we are still here carrying on the contest against the hosts of annihilation proves that on the whole the battle has gone for humanity. The world's great heart has proved equal to the prodigious undertaking which God set it. Rebuffed, but always persevering; self-reproached, but ever regaining faith; undaunted, tenacious, the heart of man labors towards immeasurably distant goals. Discouraged not by difficulties without, or the anguish of ages within, the heart listens to the secret voice that whispers: "Be not dismayed; in the future lies the Promised Land."

—Helen Keller
writer and activist

Cowards die many times before their deaths;
the valiant never taste of death but once.

—William Shakespeare
poet and playwright

Far better is it to dare mighty things, to win glorious triumphs, even though checkered by failure, than to take rank with those poor spirits who neither enjoy nor suffer much, because they live in the gray twilight that knows neither victory nor defeat.

—Theodore Roosevelt
former United States president

You gain strength, courage, and confidence by every experience in which you really stop to look fear in the face. You must do the thing which you think you cannot do.

—Eleanor Roosevelt
activist and public speaker

Bravery is being the only one who knows you're afraid.

—Franklin P. Jones
businessman

Cleanliness

No matter how soiled one's clothes may be, no matter how grimy one's face may look, the ground around the campfire must be clean, and the cooking utensils and fire wood, pot-hooks and waugan-sticks, all orderly and as carefully arranged as if the military officer was expected the next minute to make an inspection.

All my readers must remember that BY THEIR CAMPFIRE THEY WILL BE KNOWN and "sized-up" as the real thing or as chumps, duffers, tenderfeet, and cheechakos, by the first Sourdough or old-timer who cuts their trails.

—Daniel Carter Beard
co-founder of the Boy Scouts of America

The Clean Teepee and the Dirty Teepee

When my people moved into a new place, each family would be allocated a certain part of the camp to look after. They would set up their teepee or teepees. They would construct their own fire for cooking. They would have to care for the entire area under their control.

On one occasion I remember an argument between two families. It was about a certain bush. One said it was in their territory and so they could use it to hang their washing on, and the other said no, it was theirs. It was indeed a petty argument.

Aim above
morality.
Be not
simply good,
but good
for
something.

—Henry David Thoreau
writer and environmentalist

However, there were deeper causes for this argument. In the past these people had argued amongst themselves over other things. One of the families was very clean and tidy. They would always be the first at the river for morning ablutions. There would never be loose stones lying around their teepee. Their drying plants would be arranged in tidy rows, hanging on ropes. Their teepee would never be torn or dirty looking. The other family, on the other hand, was very different. They would be last for ablutions, if they were there at all. They would never all have a wash on the same day. Some days two out of the given members would wash, other days, none. They were a foul-smelling bunch. People used to castigate them for their bad habits and every so often one of them would get hurled into the river. The ground around their teepee was never swept, so that the stones would hurt peoples' feet if they walked by.

At the time when the two families were arguing about the bush for drying their clothes, we were in a camp where there was not really enough space for everyone to spread and to have their own privacy. People were irritating each other. The chief was having a hard time keeping the peace. The main reason that the clean family objected to the dirty ones was not on account of the small tree, but because they smelled so bad. Their teepee smelled bad too and the clean family was just downwind of the offending tent.

The argument grew heated. The chief had to come and mediate. When he had heard both sides of the story and had inspected both of the teepees and the surroundings of the two families, he sat down halfway between the two tents.

"I shall let my senses be the judge of this argument," he said.

"As I sit here, I am aware of the tent over there even if I close my eyes. I can smell it. I am aware of the tent over there if I walk round with my eyes closed, because I stumble on the stones scattered around it. I am aware of the family which lives in that teepee over there, because even with my back turned upon them I can smell them. They are clearly not following

The
only
reward
of virtue
is
virtue.

—RALPH WALDO EMERSON
PHILOSOPHER, POET, AND ESSAYIST

the laws of the Great Spirit with regard to cleanliness. I ask myself how I can help these people to tread on the correct path, the proper way, the way of the Great Spirit. The answer is this: I feel that if only they had a little bush to hang their dirty clothes upon, they would be able to wash their bodies and their clothes. They would also be able to clean the tent and wash the cleaning skins and hang them out to dry. It is clearly because they do not have this bush to dry their washed clothes upon, that they are such a smelly, dirty family. So I think they should have the bush. The clean family will have to set up a rope and some sticks to dry their clothes upon. I expect they will arrange their washing in a very beautiful design."

With that the chief stood up, the dirty family looking very embarrassed and the clean family looking rather bemused.

"Carry on, my children," said the old man. "The Great Spirit enjoys the sweet smell of cleanliness. See what you can do to provide it for Him!"

—Calling Horse
Indian leader

A person might be an expert in any field of knowledge or a master of many material skills and accomplishments. But without inner cleanliness his brain is a desert waste.

—Sri Sathya Sai Baba
spiritual leader

See that each hour's feelings and thoughts and actions are pure and true; then your life will be, also.

—Henry Ward Beecher
clergyman and activist

Reverence

One thing I have desired of the Lord, that will I seek after; that I may dwell in the house of the Lord all the days of my life, to behold the beauty of the Lord and to inquire in his temple.

For in the time of trouble he shall hide me in his pavilion: in the secret of his tabernacle shall he hide me; he shall set me up upon a rock.

And now shall mine head be lifted up above mine enemies roundabout me: therefore will I offer in his tabernacle sacrifices of joy: I will sing, yea, I will sing praises unto the Lord.

—Psalm 27:4-6

Do not disregard Sunday, but make it a day without offense to others whose faith may differ from yours. Give each boy an opportunity for personal devotions.

—C. B. Horton

The strength
of a man
consists
in finding out
the way
God is going,
and going
that way.

—HENRY WARD BEECHER
CLERGYMAN AND ACTIVIST

from *Te Deum*

We praise thee, O God: we acknowledge Thee to be the
    Lord.
All the earth doth worship Thee and the Father everlasting.
To Thee all Angels:
To Thee the heavens and all the powers therein.
To Thee the Cherubim and Seraphim cry with unceasing
    voice:
Holy, Holy, Holy: Lord God of Hosts.

**—Nicetas
clergyman**

A Stranger

A stranger stood by the old church door,
His clothes were old and worn;
His shoes were scuffed and the soles were loose,
His coat was ragged and torn.

I paused as I saw him standing there,
His hair was thin and gray;
And I wondered, "Should I ask this man
To come with me to pray?"

So I went to his side and softly asked,
"Old man, what is your name?"
Then he answered me and turned around
And I noticed he was lame.

His foot was red and swollen
And I thought of the pain he bore,
But he said not a word of his worry or pain
As together we stepped through the door.

We sat in the back of the old white church
And bowed our heads to pray,
But he rose after staying less than an hour,
Explaining he could not stay.

I quickly rose to follow my friend,
But when I reached the door
The man was gone, vanished from sight,
And I thought I would see him no more.

But there he was on the step of the church
So I went to him and I said,
"Old man, why can you linger not?
And I watched as he bowed his head.

"This is a house of worship.
It's God's own house, you say:
You teach that He is with you all,
That He listens while you pray.

"We love Thy house, O Lord," you sing
In loud and joyous strains,
But His sweet spirit does not dwell
Where such irreverence reigns.

"Folks giggle, whisper, laugh, and talk
In God's own house of prayer,
And when the people act this way
His spirit is not there.

Let parents
then bequeath
to their
children
not riches,
but the spirit
of reverence.

—PLATO
PHILOSOPHER

He rose and left me all alone,
And I watched as he walked the road,
And realized he had come to church
To ease his heavy load.

But once again he's left unhelped
His sorrow even more,
And I thought how right that man had been
As I listened at the door.

The noise and whispers from within
Now reached my open ears,
And suddenly I realized that
I hadn't listened in years.

I'll never forget that way I felt
As I stood at the door on that day
And listened, while unknown to them
Through irreverence they drove God away.

Since that day forth I've asked this prayer
And maybe you should, too,
"Dear Father in Heaven, please help us all
To show more reverence to you."

—Anonymous

Famous Scouts

John F. Kennedy (1917–1963), the thirty-fifth President of the United States, remains one of the most popular presidents in American history. At his inauguration ceremony he said, "Ask not what your country can do for you; ask what you can do for your country."

Henry Louis "Hank" Aaron (born 1934) was the first Major League Baseball player to hit five hundred home runs and reach three thousand hits, and for twenty-two years he held the record for the most home runs in a career. He is consistently named one of the greatest baseball players of all time.

After becoming the first person to set foot on the moon, Neil Armstrong (born 1930) said these famous words: "That's one small step for man, one giant leap for mankind."

Prior to serving as thirty-fourth President of the United States, Dwight D. Eisenhower (1890–1969) was Supreme Commander of the Allied forces in Europe during World War II. He was responsible for planning and carrying out the Allied invasion of Germany, which ultimately led to the liberation of Western Europe and the end of the Nazi regime.

Actor Harrison Ford (born 1942), best known for his role as Han Solo in the original *Star Wars* trilogy and as Indiana Jones in the series of the same name, is one of the top movie stars of all time.

In Scouting,
a boy is
encouraged
to educate
himself
instead of
being
instructed.

—ROBERT BADEN-POWELL
CO-FOUNDER OF
THE BOY SCOUTS OF AMERICA

Before gaining worldwide fame as a member of The Beatles and being knighted by the Queen of England, Sir Paul McCartney (born 1942) was a member of the Scouts in the United Kingdom.

Theodore Roosevelt (1858–1919), twenty-sixth President of the United States, greatly expanded the role of government in preserving America's natural heritage through protection of wildlife and wild areas and the foundation of the U.S. Forest Service. He was an enthusiastic supporter of the Boy Scout movement.

Wallace Stegner (1909–1993) was an influential novelist, historian, and environmentalist. His *Angle of Repose* won the Pulitzer Price for Fiction in 1972. A few years earlier, he composed his renowned "Wilderness Letter," which passionately speaks to the importance of preserving wild nature in the midst of an increasingly industrial society. "We simply need that wild country available to us," Stegner wrote. "For it can be a means of reassuring ourselves of our sanity as creatures, a part of the geography of hope."